The Best Damn

Google SEO

Book

Search Engine Optimization Techniques that
will Increase your Search Engine Ranking!

By

Heather J. Lovely

HeatherLovely.Info

The Best Damn GOOGLE SEO BOOK

LIMIT OF LIABILITY / DISCLAIMER OF WARRANTY:

The Author makes no representations or warranties regarding the accuracy or completeness of the contents of this work. The advice, theories, and strategies listed in this book may NOT be suitable for all situations and are the **sole opinion** of the Author. Any use of this information in violation of any federal, state or local law is prohibited. All trademarks, trade names, services marks and logos referenced herein belong to their respective companies.

The Best Damn GOOGLE SEO Book

Table of Contents

www.HeatherLovely.Info

Preface

In this book the topic of Search Engine Optimization will be completely analyzed and also broken down into easier parts for any average reader to be able to understand. SEO, Search Engine Optimization, is not as confusing as most people think. If a person is able to make a website or even understand how websites are made, the basic concepts of SEO can be learned by anyone. We will be discussing how SEO came into the making and how it has changed over time. Along with the various changes and differences that have occurred within SEO, there are also newer and better techniques to go along in order to optimize the ranking of your website.

One of the main things that will be discussed throughout this e-book is how to use these techniques as a whole in order to get the desired results.

By getting the desired results that you may seek, not only are you advertising your website in the "new" way, but you are also advertising the content and making the information available on your website for anyone and every user of the internet to be able to read it.

By defining how SEO really works and breaking apart the myths from the facts, the past from the present, you too can learn how to change your website according to the new standards set by most search engines.

Many people wonder what these techniques are, and some even follow them religiously. The main part which they forget is to use them as a collective instead of using them individually. We will be discussing each and every technique on its own and along with advice as to how you can accomplish that technique, and then advising as to how you can do all of them collectively starting today.

What is SEO?

Websites have been using different methods to attract the maximum number of users. For that reason, search engines have been playing a vital role in promoting these websites. Previously search engines had to rely heavily on the information provided by webmasters for that specific website. The usual factors that played a major role were: the information including keywords, index files, and Meta tags. However, the process was not that effective, as the meta data provided was not relevant to every website. Besides that, webmasters have been chaining the HTML of websites in order to rank them higher in the search engine results listing. Consequently, websites ended appearing in irrelevant search engines and for irrelevant search results. Therefore, websites were unable to generate traffic even after spending money for it.

Search engines had to design a method which can produce the desired result for the websites. Unlike previous versions of search engines, which employed irrelevant keywords in the content of the websites without proper logic, the demand for new search engines grew with many factors playing a major role.

6

With the launch of the first search engine, it was realized that the success of search engines can only be granted if it manages to produce relevant results for the search. Also, if the search engine provides the searchers with false results, they are most likely to shift to other search options. Therefore, search engines devised more complicated and lengthy processes to ensure the ranking of the website; this decreased the influence of webmasters on the overall ranking of the websites.

Furthermore, to make the ranking process solely under the control of search engines, search engines were designed with mathematical algorithms to ensure the ranking of relevant pages was devised. These search engines ranked the website on the basis of its "Page Rank".

The higher the Page Rank of the website increased was directly proportional to the ability of the website to be noticed by random searchers.

The idea was then further purified when Google was founded in 1981. Google was founded by the founder of this idea, two graduate students from Harvard University. Initially, Google became famous due to its simple design and most relevant search results.

7

To ensure the performance of the search engine, Google accounted both off-page and on-page factors of the websites. Off-page factors included the Page rank, which was the mathematical algorithm for the websites and hyperlink analysis. Besides the usual factors like keyword frequency, keyword density, Meta tags, links, site structure, and headings were analyzed as the on-page factors.

This helped the Google search engine to eliminate the manipulation by webmasters and to produce the relevant search results. However, search engines then included age, location, sex, and previous search history as off-page factors. This approach further supported the search engines to filter their results and to provide with more accurate search results. This evolution of search engines formed the base of search engine optimization, which is the most advanced method to rank the websites in the listing of search engines.

SEO stands for search engine optimization and is a method to increase the traffic on any website. It is a legal method to place the website on several different search engines.

As most of the internet searchers go for the fist few links of the search result. SEO takes the website to the highest position in the search results, so that the searchers can click the specific website to fulfill their needs. Besides, it offers the website links to other websites for the purpose of bringing new users to the website.

Search engine optimization employs a tool called "spider", which is used to get information about the updated websites on the internet. When a page is updated the spider provides the information about the words, videos, images, and other relevant content on the webpage which has been changed. However, spider can only recognize and judge words; therefore, the nature of images, video, and images is not recognized by the spider. On a positive note, it updates the search engine by providing the tags for videos and images. These tags provide the accurate information and description of the image and videos. So that when the searcher looks for those specific key words, the search engine can provide them with the most relevant results. These words are called the "key words".

Most of the people consider search engine optimization as only the game of key words. However, it is more than that, as it makes use of Meta tags and hyperlinks besides the key words.

For the purpose of understanding, keyword is taken as the only factor to be incorporated by SEO. However, in technical terms, there is lot more that a search engine optimization company does in order to bring the websites to highest ranking of the search engine. The density of keywords in the overall content of the website increases the possibility of the website to be listed higher in the listing of search results.

Search engine optimization also demands high level of care while using keywords in the content of the website. Website's that are overcrowded with the keywords can be ignored by the spider, as the spider has a defined tolerance level for keywords. If any page exceeds the tolerance level of the spider it is most likely to get banned from the search engine just so that it does not appear in the search results at all. Therefore, it is recommended to use keywords between 2% to 7% of the whole content. However, if the content of the website is well managed and comply with quality standards 12% keywords density can also be used. Spider also takes feedback from the title, headings, links, and Meta tags used in the website; therefore, websites can use keywords in these so as to get noticed by the spider.

However, people focus more on the outlook of the website, neglecting the optimization aspect of the website. Therefore, while developing the websites one of the important factors to be taken into consideration for optimization is being able to support the specific codes. The website is made to provide the specific needs of researchers by being able to provide them the experienced and high quality content. However, it should be designed keeping in view all the factors considered by the spider.

Basic SEO Tips

Search engine optimization is a whole process which many people get confused as to how they can use it effectively and thus they get their websites banned from the search engines due to the lack of knowledge. To resolve this issue, websites should be designed with a balanced approach while being created. However, there are some tips that might be helpful for you to keep in mind in order to achieve top notch desired SEO results. These include:

The Title of Websites

While getting feedback from the website, the spider of most search engines goes for the title of the website first. The title is the bar at the up-most part of the screen which holds the name of the website; it is also called the "title bar" of the website. Therefore, it is necessary to include important keywords in the title of the website. The title has to be short and simple, yet descriptive enough to provide the keyword or information about the website.

Search engines use the title of websites in order to provide basic information to the searcher; therefore, it has to be captivating enough to be clicked by the user.

Furthermore, it is advised to use the keywords in the body of the website. Irrelevant or different keywords cannot produce the desired results which the webmaster wants attain through the search engine results. However, to ensure the optimization for a specific website the usage of different keywords for each separate page of the website is highly important. Otherwise the spider will consider all the pages exactly the same and thus consequently, the website will not be listed in the search engine index.

Keywords to be used

Keywords are one of the main factors of search engine optimization; therefore, in order to achieve the highest in the natural listing of the search engine results you have to be careful to use the appropriate keywords.

People mostly overuse keywords for search engine optimization; however their density should not increase from 2% to 7% otherwise the spider starts to ignore the website. It is important not to try and stuff keywords in every place and situation throughout the website. Keywords have to be accurate and relevant to the place where they are used. It is recommended to use secondary and tertiary keywords as well. These are different keywords; however they stand close to the main keywords as in their meanings.

Due to the diverse use of keywords, websites are allowed to use different techniques regarding keywords.

Using one keyword can be ineffective as well, as people use combinations of different words while searching. Therefore, it is recommended to identify the best combination of keywords that can be used in the content of website to bring more traffic to the page.

Google search engine's spider searches the first few sentences of the paragraph to find the relevant keywords. Therefore, in order to rank highest in search engine results of most search engines, it is advised to use the keywords in the first paragraph.

Links

It is observed that websites which are referred as quality websites often deliver quality information and services as compared to other websites. Similarly, these links on the websites are taken as the positive points for that websites, by the search engine spider. Therefore, more quality links on the website increase its ability to be ranked higher in the Google search results.

Linking websites to link-farms can produce adverse effects for your website. Therefore, quality should not be compromised whiling linking the website to other relevant websites.

Besides, the website can get support from other websites if it promises to deliver the quality content to its visitors. Other websites take pride in referring to other quality and original websites as well.

Meta tags

Meta tags are HTML embedded elements; these tags provide information about the data on the websites. Data about the description of the page, keywords, and other informational content that does not appear on the website is provided by the Meta tags. Meta tags are also key elements of the website to be used for search engine optimization. However, these tags are not as effective when they are used alone.

Google search engine's robot uses Meta tags to identify and categorize the websites. Therefore, these tags cannot be skipped being the vital part of search engine optimization.

15

Keywords

Meta keyword attributes are used to employ the keywords used in the body of the website in the meta-elements of the websites. There is no consensus about the effectiveness of Meta keywords of the websites. There is one school of thought that supports the use of Meta keywords attributes; however, at the same time there are professionals who deny the effectiveness of the Meta keyword attributes.

Description

The description attribute of the Meta tags is used to provide the explanation of the content of the website. Description attributes are appreciated by almost every professional and is seen as the most effective Meta tag to be used. Keywords are used in this description specifically to increase the ranking of the website through the search results.

However, some keywords used in the content are employed in the Meta description tag of the website.

It is used by search engines as a brief overview of the page while providing the link to the searcher.

www.HeatherLovely.Info

Therefore, it provides an opportunity to the website to get the maximum traffic if the description is attractive.

Language

The language attribute of the Meta tags is used to define the language in which the content is written. It does not talk about the coding language of the website, rather the language of the content. However, these Meta tags cannot be used to include keywords; still they provide great help to the search engine in deciding the language of the website, so that they can provide the links to the relevant user.

Robots

These Meta tags are used to facilitate the spider of Google's search engine.

These tags tell the spider either to index the page or not. Similarly, No follow used a robot attribute of Meta Tags which prevent the link from being crawled. Besides, there are several other attributes of the Meta tags that can be used facilitate the spider of the search engine.

Search engine optimization makes use of almost all of these Meta tags. However, keywords and description attributes of Meta tags are used more commonly than any other form.

17

People make use of robot attributes in order to facilitate the spider; however, they neglect the human aspect of websites. Google's spider can even ban the website from the search engine if the website is missing the human element in it.

SEO Content

Search engine optimization is an extremely long process and has many factors which come into play. These methods, like SEO Content, are especially designed to help increase the amount of traffic visiting your website. By updating and keeping these online marketing techniques, one can easily keeps the traffic flowing towards the website and get visitors to involved. Some of the have to do with how often the website is updated, how many other websites are linking to your website, and whether or not all of the websites and links on your website are properly working or not. There are some other things which you can actually have a direct influence on, which is where SEO content comes into play.

Depending on the relevance of the content that is on your web page, the ranking of your web site is raised in search engines as well as other online directories.

Along with the content that is placed on your website, the conditions of the Meta tags which are placed on your website play a major role.

This idea of having your content quality higher than the quantity is what really matters. The higher quality of website that you have to offer to your consumers and viewers, the higher quality search engine results and rankings will be achieved. It will attract attention; it has proven to do so. It will not only gain attention of consumers but also have other web page creators using links directing to your webpage as well as other types of referrals. These things build up the ranking of the website, and over the period of time all these factors start playing an important role and help raise the ranking of the website.

The more natural type of business you can get the more positive results you will be achieving naturally. Keep in mind to be genuine and unique as well as planning on staying a long time while keeping up with competition.

One of the best ways to get your website ranking in the top 10 is the content that your website provides.

This is considered as one of the biggest changes that have occurred in the search engine results over the last few years, the change in the content of a website. Increasing your content will help increase your website to get to the desired place you want to be. The challenge is to keep a balance between quality and quantity of the content.

Quantity & Quality

The change in quantity versus quality has also occurred recently as there has been a decline in web pages that have started resembling to look like brochures or just magazine ads.

These websites have proven to be ineffective when it comes to search engine optimization and for marketing purposes as well. In order to have your website be ranked at a higher position, the quality of the content is extremely important. This fact can be verified due to the statistics that have been provided by such websites, like GoRank.com. GoRank.com has stated that the average words that are appearing on a Yahoo search are usually pages that have more than 1,300 words on an average, when compared to Google's results of having around 940 words per page. These results are just results which have been given for searches that have came back in the top 10.

Most website owners do not want to invest a lot of money into advertising programs which require tons of money. There are nearly two major solutions to help getting your website receive a higher location when searched for.

You can either hire a team of professional copywriters that can easily develop some attracting and powerful content for your specific website's needs, or you can learn to do these techniques yourself. Obviously starting up yourself will require much more, besides the cost of getting professional copywriters to help you improve the position of your website is worth it in the end.

Professional Tips regarding SEO Content

Professional copy writers have learned the techniques needed to develop quality content versus quantity content. They have experienced and learned the techniques of developing excelling quality marketing content, while using the basic fundamentals of many other SEO techniques. There needs to be a lot involved in building content while keeping those fundamental SEO techniques in mind.

For instance, search engines usually return results to people who search for keywords in the exact order of relevancy. The more relevant the site may seem to those keywords when searched for; your listing will automatically start to appear higher. Obviously some people think of this as being simple and adding and repeating the same key phrase over and over may increase the listing's position, but it is not that easy.

Google's search engine has said to analyze the page content before listing it. Instead of the simple scan through the website for that specific keyword in the text of the website, Google's technology analyzes the entire content of the page. There are many factors that come into affect when it searches for these, such as the different fonts used, the sub divisions, as well as the locations of each word. This is how Google determines the relevancy of the website to the user's search query.

Another thing that Google does in order to ensure quality of returned results is to analyze the content of other web pages in order to determine an "overall" position of your website.

SEO Content also aids in the "stemming" of words. Stemming is when searching for a part of the word; the whole thing might come up. For instance, if you were to search for 'drinking', it would be linked to the stem word drink. It creates a better chance for people to be able to see more content. The key is not to use the exact key phrase over and over again but to actually break it down throughout the entire content. Within the content, it should be used separately and broken apart to create more results.

Using the same key phrase over and over again may in fact lower the rating of a website, but using the key phrase broken apart throughout the content is an easy way to raise the awareness.

Blending in other words and using the "stemming" option is extremely helpful and beneficial in raising the listing of your website. However, it is still important to use that key phrase throughout the article in order to make sure that it gets picked up. It should be spread apart from the beginning, middle, and the end of the entire content to make sure it gets picked up in a positive manner.

The relevant keyword density within the article should be well maintained according to the content of the article as well in order to maintain a high quality content based website. By keeping with the theme of the article, and using those tricks mentioned above with SEO Content one can achieve great results throughout search engines, especially Google's search engine.

Non-Content Sites using SEO Content

Many different website owners have the complaint that their website is not a website which is based off of content.

This is a major disadvantage, even to business websites. Having a non-content type of website, even for a business, is already making your website similar to other websites. When it is similar to other websites available throughout the internet, especially through Google's search results, there is no way of attracting customers to your website. In order for customers to be attracted to your website, they must first be able to find your website with ease through search results.

The solution is to be creative and think outside the box. Any topic and every topic can have at least something written about it by anyone; even if it is just basic information.

If you end up selling some type of flooring on your website, by writing content as to what the differences are in flooring you are able to attract customers easily. Even if your prices are higher than other competition, you can easily attract them online by having basic information which the average consumer can use to their advantage. Having a comparison of different types of flooring is one example. Having advice as to how to take care of the flooring or how to prepare for getting your house remodeled is another example. Generally speaking, by doing a little bit of research out of your own time and you can generate ideas and maybe even write the history of such flooring in an interesting format. Although you might think at first that this is silly and it will not help increase the number of people that visit your website, but the fact is that when they search for these things off of Google's search engine, your website will be one which already all the information gathered on one location in a unique, entertaining, and creative manner.

The Catch

However, here's the catch. This type of marketing through SEO Content is mostly used for websites which can actually deliver a large amount of quantity of any specific type of content.

The more specific and unique type of quantity that the website can provide to the people surfing, the better the chances can be for their website being a top result as one.

The best way to do that is to have your website offering information in a unique way about unique things which cannot be found on other websites. That way, the competition is extremely low since your website will be offering information. The chances of you being placed highly in the search engine response page are extremely high.

If the content on your website is something which is very popular and can easily be found throughout the search engine responses, much more dedication and hard work will be required on your part. It is difficult to place high on a search engine response page, or SERP, through just the quality or quantity of content and other factors come into place. The point is that even with heavy competition or no heavy competition, SEO content is an important factor in deciding the placement of your website on search engine results.

Other factors excluded, SEO content alone is a major benefiting point to your website at a high level of degree, but you cannot count on it to place your website as one of the top most ranking websites on Google's search results.

Overall

The basic understanding of content based SEO is extremely easy to understand in the initial stages. It might seem difficult to start, but once the wheel starts rotating it is extremely easy to make sure rotates in a way that benefits your website as well as the number of visitors to your website. Content on your website is one of the best and easiest ways to simply benefit your website in the most stable and best way to achieve long-term results. Once the wheel is spinning, the content on your website is extremely easy to maintain and to keep putting up new content while polishing up the old content.

Many people make a simple mistake and think that there is no difference between SEO content and optimized content.

The fact is that they both are very similar and go hand in hand. SEO Content means search engine optimization through content.

If the website you provide to viewers is already heavily flowing through content, your website is automatically optimized for search engines. Google's search engine will especially love to provide your website to other viewers; which in fact gives you a higher ranking compared to other websites.

When you start to provide content on your website which is unique and original, not only are you writing in a format which includes keywords that will help optimize your content, but you are also able to fill in the missing attributes for the Meta tags on your website. The SEO content that is provided on your website is just part of it, but you should also be very familiar with different HTML and CSS commands as well in order to better use the content available on your website. Knowing the basics of HTML can improve the overall performance of your website.

The quality of your content is extremely important as many of the popular search engines start to rank websites according to the quality that is provided on their website. By having extremely well written content on your website is a sure way of getting ranked higher than other websites throughout the search engine results, especially throughout Google's search engine results.

Maintaining a decent density of popular keywords throughout your content is a sure way of maintaining quality while keeping your content unique. It is up to your preference to choose what may be more benefiting for your website, but usually having a 10% density within the content is a sure way of making your content better. 10% density means that out of 100 words, at most 10 of those words are the popular key words that are searched for.

SEO Link Building

SEO Link Building is an extremely important part of optimizing your search results throughout the various search engines, especially through Google's search engine. Many people do not consider it to be important when it comes to ranking, but the truth is that the link building factor is an extremely decisive factor in determining whether or not your website actually makes it or does not. Links between websites are an essential part of the internet, especially through HTTP protocol, and HTTP protocol is not getting replaced anytime soon. Investing a lot of time in this determining factor is important and is worth the time spent learning in the end.

However, this does not mean that you can place all types of links throughout your website and get discouraged when your website isn't ranked highly on search engines.

Google's search engine has now become so advanced and elegant that it cannot differentiate between the links which actually matter and are verified and trusted links versus those links that should not count.

Many factors fall into the verification of a link, mainly the domain age and the user data are important, along with many others. Google's search engine really knows how to optimize and provide results through the links that are provided on a website, whereas other search engines are not able to do it like Google has. I will be discussing the different techniques that fall under link building and have to do with search engine optimization.

Link Building Tip #1

Lists

The first step is to actually build a list of a type. People love to read lists that can provide them simple information in a simple manner.

These also get linked to very commonly, meaning your website gets linked to more often if you are able to provide some type of list of information. For example, an article on a "list of 10 easy ways to list building" is very common and an easy way of having other websites link to your website for information. As long as the information provided in that article is unique and actually worth reading.

Overall, having any type of list provided on your website is a sure way of attracting viewers as well as other webmasters throughout the internet. Lists are easy to read and do not require as much time to follow through with. People love lists to gather information quickly and efficiently.

Link Building Tip #2
Link Building

Before starting this topic, let's just start with our intentions. Our intention behind link building is not to be competitive but to be available to other users with ease and comfort.

By relating to other webmasters and referring to other important figures and sites is an easy way of link building. This is one of the oldest methods used by webmaster in order to improve link popularity. The way to do it is to get in touch with other website owners who also contain information which is similar to yours and work together as a team in order to pursue higher search engine results. The best way to do it is to talk to other websites that are not competing with you for a higher position, but rather very similar to yours. Of course you can always pre-qualify these websites to see if they might even be interested in your offer if they have similar links on their website like you proposed.

33

You start off with contacting the webmaster and discuss the mutual benefits of linking to and from one another's websites. In order to do this, you must have original and unique content on your website that others may want to share as well.

It is an extremely factor to discuss everything in detail, including what the link will say and what will be the position of the link so it is mutually understood from the beginning. You have to think win\win and compromise to achieve results. In order to make yourself seem important and different from other users, you must contact them in a manner which is different. Different in the sense of writing a letter and mailing it or calling them in order to show the amount of dedication and motivation you have.

The best way to do this is to search for keywords which are similar to your website and to contact all the resultants. It is important not to get discouraged if many people do not see eye to eye with you on this topic, but those who will see eye to eye with you will be benefiting with you as much as you will be.

Having a link for the other website already on your website is often hard to say No to by other webmasters and delivers better responses when they see you actually taking some initiative. Communicating verbally delivers much better results than a simple email.

Of course there are other methods of building links. Some of the extremely easy but t he most productive type of link building is to advertise your website online. Advertising it on other websites, such as forums which may have users asking questions which you may already have an answer for on your website. Providing answers to major groups or question boards is an easy way to build resources and creating a flow of traffic to your website. Advertising your website through other websites is the basic concept of link building, and is extremely important.

You can easily do it and it will provide you a great amount of desired results only for sacrificing some time to build some rapport of your website.

One other way of people commonly advertising their website is by providing their website link in their signatures.

Link Building Tip #3
Hire Help

By hiring a professional consultant or professional help to aid you in link building is an easy way. All it takes is a little bit of money, a little bit of investment, and you are already starting to grow your website. Outsourcing link building is a very common type of technique used by major important website owners. It is important to recommend someone who is good and knows all about search engine optimization.

The web is changing continuously, especially the way people are receiving information on a daily basis.

In order to keep up with this rapid change, the best way is to actually get some help from someone who does this for a living.

By getting help with the design and overall scheme of the website can totally change the outlook of your website. It can change the way viewers perceive the website as well as the way they are able to use it.

36

People love to get information from an easy and verified source, if you can provide both of those to the average viewer; Google's search engine will automatically start tracking your website and ranking it higher.

Some websites go as far as to hiring a professional public relations manager. This can aide in getting the word out of your website as well as what your overall goals are. This can attract the local community and society and maybe even the overall population of a country.

Link Building Tip #4
Becoming Socially Interactive

In order to be attractive for other viewers when searched for, your website must include a recent update of content which has to do with recent events that have taken place. Important events are something which most people want more information right away. If they can receive it all from one source, one source which provides it in a creative and unique manner, then the website is already above other websites. Attracting others by being socially interactive is a very important factor of link building.

If you can provide constant updates or recent updates which have to do with local or a whole society, then you may already be getting linked to by other websites. Becoming socially interactive is an important way of developing traffic of viewers from other websites as they will right away attract to you.

By being socially interactive, you can provide and extend your website as a means of information to travel easier. Interesting interviews can be taken place and also be put up in an original and unique manner. Information has always spread like the speed of light, as people love to gossip. Gossip can be your friend when you have a website that is giving informative details about social events which affect a large number of people.

Link Building Tip #5
Free Stuff

Most people are always interested in trying to gain something for doing as less amount of work possible. The best way to encourage and motivate people to do something is to have some type of prize to offer. The best prize can be in monetary terms.

Even if you create a type of content of some sort with a cash prize, the amount you will be investing into your own website is worth it when you see the worth and value of what you actually accomplished without actually doing anything.

By giving out free stuff easily and openly, you will not only be increasing the traffic of your website through advertising, but also getting the ranking of your website higher during search engine results.

SEO Video Marketing

Search Engine optimization has gone a long way, especially with the new video market which has been created recently. Video Optimization is a great way in order to deliver news and information about your products or services in a new and unique manner. As technology is rapidly increasing over and over, so are the ways people are searching for tools. Google has updated to a Universal Search, which displays video results for search inquiries. Like with every new technique that has come out, it has stuck around for a very long time, and the same is expected to happen with Video Marketing.

Videos are a great way to intercept and contact their target markets and get the message through easily. A great fact that we all can witness easily is the amount of advertising we have seen ourselves when we're surfing the internet. We see many video's popping up and trying to attract and deliver a specific message.
Like all other technique used for SEO, video marketing has a lot of techniques as well.

One of the most important things with video marketing is to make sure that the clips that you have made are relevant, somewhat unique, as well as informative.

40

It must demonstrate maturity and a sense of intelligence throughout the video while maintain a level of comedy and humor. It is important to keep an updated collection while making sure and avoiding confusing your audience. Upload a video only if you actually feel it to be worth the time of other viewers, otherwise you will already start gaining negative reviews.

Titles are an important part of SEO, and just like all other materials of SEO, video marketing requires attractive titles to be picked up search engine robots. By having an extremely catchy title for either content or articles or even the videos on your website, you will surely be attracting customers surfing the internet.

Like all other catchy titles, you must have the keywords in your title in order to attract people searching for that specific keyword.

Having a type of logo or a symbol on your videos is a great of differentiating your videos from other people's video.

Along with a logo you may want to only keep a certain amount of time dedicated to your videos. For instance videos that are too long may seem boring or uninteresting for people as they only have a few minutes to spend.

Whatever videos you may put up, you must try to make it less than five minutes in order to attract viewers instantly.

Another major important factor to keep in mind when uploading videos is something that can be done easily. It is to make sure that there is a lot of basic html surrounding it. The content around the video should have key phrases regarding the video in order for it to better serve and increase the ranking on search engine results.

SEO Bookmarking

The basic understanding or fundamental behind search engine optimization is to actually advertise your website to the ordinary person. The reason to do this is so when the person searches a specific keyword or key string in Google's search engine; it automatically starts to display websites in an order which is not random. The order is determined by many different factors which have been covered throughout this e-book. The best way to get your website at a higher ranking, like discussed throughout, is to advertise and publicize your website to the average reader. SEO Bookmarking is a very common and useful strategy used by many of the great webmasters throughout the World Wide Web.

Bookmarking is a type of search engine optimization in which you are advertising your website, or bookmarking it, on other websites for people to be able to get a glance of your website.

By placing your website information on a public web site which is accessible by the ordinary and average user of the internet, they can be viewed from any computer with any type of internet access.

43

The links which you may find interesting can also be easily advertised through the help of such websites. Most commonly, Digg or DeL.icio.us are two very common types of websites that are used to bookmark other websites. By being registered on these websites, one can easily share, store, and tag any type of bookmarks, even if they're yours or someone else's.

Now, for someone trying to accomplish optimization through search engines the best bet of getting the desired results is to market your website. It might be considered guerrilla marketing in some manners, but the results it provides are extremely powerful towards marketing your entire website over the internet and Google's search engines.

However, one must always be cautious as too much advertising can seem like spam and therefore divert viewers away from your website. Making the list of bookmarks attractive, unique, and easy to follow through is an extremely important factor when bookmarking. Overall, this whole process takes only a little bit of time as you have to only register with these public websites, and then you can start listing away.

Starting Up

There are a number of websites that have been created with the sole purpose of being used for sharing interesting links and bookmarking articles. By doing a simple search online, one can find a number of websites that have to offer different and unique things. But before starting up on a website, there is usually a very similar list of requirements in order to start up at a social bookmarking website.

First of all, what you need to be able to provide is some type of content full of value.

The content must be creative, attractive, and unique as well as something which someone may just want to read. Although the quality of the content is extremely important, the next major topic to cover is the title that is used to describe that content. The title must be simple, but while being simple and short, it has to be informative about what the entire article talks about, why it is different, as well as extremely attractive. The keyword's which have been used throughout the content must be used at least once in the title. You will also find it handy to find a tool which can monitor all of your accounts as well as keep statistics and a detailed analysis of the links which you can use to your own advantage.

One of the things which you can do, either when starting up or after you have started up is to use a keyword which is extremely unique within the title or content. Have that keyword set up to alert you or notify you as soon as it starts getting bookmarked to, or linked to. This little test can show you the effectiveness and the spread of bookmarking.

It is an extremely cost effective method to create a network of web for you which is very well maintained and indexed thoroughly. However, one of the biggest problems with this method is the amount of time it may take for a person to set everything up, and to get past spam detectors if the content and the title are something realistic and original. If spam detectors take it as a piece of spam, they will automatically delete it.

Many people who surf the internet often see buttons and links on some websites which are similar to "Delic.io.us", or "Digg this", like those two there are many more which can be used for bookmarking. The main purpose of a SEO Bookmarking website is to tell other members what one may have seen, enjoyed, and felt the need to share it with other viewers as well. This is a dream come through for people trying to raise their website through people searching for keywords.

By being able to get a few people of a part of a community together and coming towards your website, they will generate more traffic than you can imagine. The word will spread through the community and people will be intrigued to find out more by visiting more people visiting often to your website.

Many people feel as though their content is so diverse that it would have no place on a website like this, but the truth is far from that. These are communities full of people from all over the word and the topics which you provide can be virtually categorized into any topic. By doing so, people will be expecting something unique when they go into that category of the website. This in return proves to them that your website does have a variety of topics.

By building different types of links that go to different topics on your website, you will be helping people finding your website. Each time you create a link which is part of the main link and then place it on a bookmarking website; you will have a link that is created in favor of you. There is no negative side to this. By building a link and then placing them on different social bookmarking websites, you will be creating as many links for yourself by each individual post on a bookmarking website.

47

Obviously the more time you invest in trying to advertise your market, the better off you'll be and the more results you get.

Bookmarking Tip #1

One of the most important things to do when submitting a list of bookmarks on such websites is to only share the ones which you feel are actually worth the time of the viewers and may gain attention right away. Bookmarking other websites which are also affiliated with your website can also be used as a diverging tool and be helpful overall. You must remember not to lie or fake a site and try to cheat someone into coming to your website because it will honestly do nothing for getting you your desired results from search engines.

Besides, theses websites are more often focused on the popularity of the user, which is gained through time and having various people agreeing the value of the bookmark placed. When people are agreeing and actually reading the material often, the popularity of your website grows which in return increases the ranking of your website on Google's search engine results.

It is important to not abuse the freedom which is given to you and start publishing every site as this can be seen as an annoyance by frequent visitors. You need to judge your own work and see which should actually be presented.

Bookmarking Tip #2

Marketing teaches us the life cycle period of a product. Your website is your product. In order to establish and start some growth, there are four major stages. In the introduction stage, you will need to actually spend a lot of time in order to get to the desired location. In the growth stage, you will actually have to spend less time than originally and already start seeing some results.

Eventually you will get your product, or website, at a maturity level where it produces results with very little work. Like all products there will be a decline period, where the demand for such a website starts to decrease. This applies to your website overall.

The fact is as simple as this: you will hit a decline stage eventually. It is how you deal with it that matters. Either you can give up or try to do something creative and unique in order to get back into the maturity level and start seeing some increase in the demand for your website.

To be able to draw a significant amount of traffic from your older bookmarks is quite common and is used by many other people. The search engine takes those links and puts it in the history, or the cached sites, and thus they are connected to your normal website for any average user searching for keywords that fit your website. Many of the social bookmarking websites that are available currently provide a type of 'dofollow' links.

Do follow links are once in which if the author has written any piece of content but titles it with the correct attracting keywords, then the users searching for these keywords through Google's search engine will directly be able to see your provided link. The external link which has been placed on such public websites must have useful and attracting keywords throughout the main link. Since other people are also continuously adding links, or bookmarking, to such public websites other traffic can also be transferred over to your solid links leading to your website. Overall, the whole transfer of traffic to your website increases the rating and the ranking within Google's search engine.

Social bookmarking, like other techniques mentioned in this book, is not meant to be used as the primary source of gathering traffic.

Along with the other techniques mentioned and put together, only then will it start to make a difference. All of these combined together have proven to provide the desired results.

SEO Article Writing

Search Engine Optimization (SEO) writing is a term that has been given various meanings and been used to define a large array of writing endeavors. It is due to this that the term has often been misinterpreted and people still consider it as a simple offshoot of article writing. However, SEO is much more than that. It differs from other forms in that it aims to provide factual and objective evidence to convince the reader about a certain topic. These can be anything from buying a specific brand of lamps to buying a specific form of mortgage.

It should be noted that writing is a unique talent which is not found commonly or inclines people towards similar topics. The skill of good writing requires not just talent but also the ability to express in a manner which seems true to the original experience. In cases where people have to write fiction, they use the same faculty but with the purpose of defining something which they have felt.

In such cases, reality gives way to fiction and people have to use imagination instead of a solid foundation of objective truth. The fact that both these experiences make use of the feelings of the person when he encountered the particular object makes both similar.

Therefore, writing in its simplest form is the ability to express a person's reactions. They may be to something that exists in reality or they may be to something completely fictional.

SEO writing is about the experiences felt when the person is considering objects and entities in real life. The writer's aim is to explain to the readers what he/she experienced while utilizing the object under discussion. The descriptive process is focused on the object, something which is very real and can be experienced by the reader as well. At the same time, it is not a document meant to list all the details of that object. It is meant to be a preliminary and brief introduction of the object aimed at garnering the reader's attention.

To excite interest among the readers, it is necessary to first know what your readers are attracted to. Key words are the barometer by which articles are rated in their scales of relevance. For instance, an article on cancer grows in relevance with words like cancer, illness and chemotherapy. The result is that readers who want to look for an article on cancer and who may have typed in any of these as the search word will be directed to the article. Key words form the main guiding principle for search engine to direct readers towards relevant articles.

53

There are many different tips and techniques to go over in order to be able to write articles properly, especially articles specifically written for the purpose of optimizing the content on your website. Some of the essential tools for writing articles for the purpose of SEO are simple but often overlooked. The first thing for beginners is to actually feel like they're writing something unique and creative.

It is often hard to think outside the box, but it is your box and you are at the liberty to move around as you wish. You are creating a unique piece of work which you are totally in charge of and you have the authority to change it as you wish. Along with that, you must start developing a love for reading. Reading every word, phrase, sentence that you see and analyzing how it is written and why it is written the way it is. You can use this technique to be creative on your own and get some tips from them or use them as a guideline of accomplishing something different.

SEO articles vary with each topic. Every topic has its specific qualities which need to be addressed. Similarly, every topic has differing levels of information which need to be explained to the reader. Therefore, some topics are easy to decipher and can be explained in a few lines.

Other topics are much more difficult and need to be explained in a more detailed manner.

However, one thing to note is that when readers are going over articles such as these, they will not have the attention span required of a long detailed essay. Readers are much more interested in acquiring the gist of the article. It is therefore necessary to focus on writing concise information. The longer the article is dragged, the harder it becomes for the reader to remain focused on the information which negates the whole point of the article.

It is necessary to look at articles as a means to convince people. SEO articles require precision and focus so that the reader is able to pick out the exact information he requires. In order to be this precise the article needs to have a precise topic as well. There is how ever one extremely important detail to keep in mind when writing a SEO article, which is that a pre-set topic can never fully explain the article. Every article evolves and changes as it is written and so a topic which one sets out to write may not be the same once it is complete.
This may lead to confusion and the readers may not be impressed by the lack of direction.

It is also necessary to spend an effective amount of time on your articles instead of writing hours on one single article. You do not have to aim for perfection when writing or while writing. Most of the articles written by famous authors and writers are not perfect the first time they write it, and then later they are made into published works. Getting the thoughts within your head out on a piece of paper is the second step towards article writing while using your time effectively. By learning this major step people can start to write tons of good stuff and eventually get to a point of having "back-up" articles written which can be revised and published during a hectic or slow time period. By getting the thoughts out, without worrying about the format, or the grammar, or even the flow of the article, you will be doing yourself a huge favor and saving a lot of time. Once you have finished getting all of your thoughts out on paper, you can move on.

Another important part of article writing is to be able to use keywords effectively in the content. The keywords that you have chosen should be placed effectively and should not be a large number in a ratio of the total words. At the most, you want to have 10% density of the keywords. Place them throughout the article in a strategic manner as well as in between sentences, but make sure that it can make sense.

While doing so, you don't have to focus too much on proofreading at this stage. Once you've completed putting in keywords throughout the article, you can move on to the next step.

At this stage you will begin to use your logic instead of creative side of the mind. You can start looking out for spelling mistakes, even though sometimes some word applications are not able to tell problems from one another. You start off correcting the grammatical mistakes as well while you're reading through, making sure to make it sound clean and crisp.

While proofreading, you can also keep adding different information regarding the topic throughout the article in order to try to perfect it. You must go through the entire article very slowly and carefully in order to make sure you don't make any silly mistakes. In order to do this effectively, I have mentioned another stage, which you can go towards while finishing this stage.

In this stage you will finalize everything. You will be re-editing and re-proofreading your topic again. You may take a few minutes, walk around, clear your mind, and come back to the content before starting this topic in order to make sure you don't make any silly mistakes. This is extremely important.

A major way of figuring out if maybe some words are misspelled or in the wrong position is to start reading the article backwards to make sure it flows. After this stage, you are ready to start publishing.

Other Techniques

Meta tags and keywords can help the website to appear higher in the listing of the Google search engine. However, it is only the website which will retain the visitor for further browsing the website. Therefore, other aspects of the website have to be considered before going towards search engine optimization. The human aspect of the website should not be ignored while developing the websites. Making websites solely for the purpose of search engine optimization can adversely affect the results. Most of the people put their focus on the technical requirements forgetting about basic requirements of a good website. This mostly becomes the reason that they get their websites banned by the Google search engine spider. Besides, the technical aspects of creating a websites, human elements should also be considered to generate the traffic on websites.

Website Design

Most of the people fail to link the website design with search engine optimization; however, websites with very bold color scheme and font are unable to be read with ease.

59

Such websites fail to grasp the attention for visitors, as there might be other better quality options available for him. Therefore, besides the technical procedure of search engine optimization, the thought of attracting users of the internet should not be ignored in its development. Mostly, websites are designed with the intention of optimization and these websites get clicked by the users as well; however, their lack of ability to retain the user for the desired period of time ruins all the efforts for search engine optimization. Also, websites with same theme or topics do not get the same preference from the spider of Google search engine optimization, as compared with other websites with different themes and topics.

Quality

Website design is used to attract the visitors; however, users do not visit the website for its design.

They demand value for the time they spent on websites; therefore, the quality of the content used in on a website has to be ensured. For that reason, it is important to use original and accurate information in the content of the website. It is seen that websites often copy the content from other websites or internet sources. In that case, visitors simply reject to consider both of the website, as both of them become unauthentic for the reader.

However, for the purpose of search engine optimization, keywords should be placed in appropriate situations throughout the content. Otherwise, content quality of the website will be affected, making the search engine optimization ineffective and working against rather than in favor of the website.

Quantity

Though, the visitor's prime focus is to get quality content from the first pages of search engine. However, if they fail to get the desired quantity of information, they are most likely to use other websites to fulfill their needs.

In that case, even the basic search engines have optimized with this factor at one point or another. However, most of the websites do not support or keep the quantity of the articles or content in mind, but still expect to get their desired results.

Modifications

It is also recommended to keep changing the content of the website regularly. There are different methods through which the content can be changed automatically. However, to reduce the technicalities it can be and should be done manually. Therefore, when the visitors find new content every time they use the website, they get more value for the time they spend on it.

61

Black hat techniques

There are several search engine optimization techniques that are ranked as black hat, which mean that they are not supported by the Google search engine. Therefore, websites using black hat techniques are often banned automatically by the Google search engine.

Doorway pages, hidden text, cloaking, identical pages, keyword fillers, very high keyword density, and mirror pages are few of the most used forms of black hat techniques.

Black hat techniques for search engine optimization can help to bring the website higher in the ranking for a very short period of time. However, these techniques do not support the long term objectives of websites. Besides, visitors do not appreciate the websites using prohibited methods to prove their quality.

Advanced SEO Techniques

Advanced SEO techniques are not different than the basic techniques; however, advanced techniques focus more on the technical aspect of search engine optimization. Almost all the advanced techniques caters the small elements associated with search engine optimization, therefore, the combined affect of these small elements produce superior results for the websites. Techniques differ according to the nature of the element they play with , however all of them follow one basic rule, which is make the website relevant in order to rank it higher in Google search results.

As the nature of these elements vary according to search engine's requirement and nature of keywords. Therefore, it is impossible to design an advanced formula for all to make search engine optimization effective. Besides, there are factors that affect the search engine optimization results along with the basic requirements of search engine optimization.
However, there are a few methods that can be modified as per requirement in order to generate the desired results.

Website maps

Google search engine spider is the only tool that indexes the website in the search engines. Therefore, it is necessary to provide as much convenience to Google spider as possible in order to achieve a higher ranking, however, the convenience level should also be provided to the humans visiting the website and not just a computerized algorithm. Spider does not allow websites to appear on the search engines which are not providing the basic and essential demands of the visitors. Therefore websites are recommended to provide the necessary information to the search engine which will facilitate the Google spider while keeping in mind and trying to help the viewers visiting your website.

Sitemap is the basic factor that the spider uses to index the website.
Therefore, it is mandatory to provide the sitemap to Google in order to facilitate the spider. These sitemaps are provided as dynamic XML files and as per the specification of Google. However it must be ensured that the visitors use the website according to the sitemap provided to Google. The sitemaps help the spider to provide information about the updated content and other relevant material.

With that, it is also important to provide the description of the photos, videos, and images with the relevant keywords describing the material used.

Working of Spiders

As spiders are the most important tools used by search engines to rank the websites, it is essential to understand the working of spiders.

Therefore for one of the advanced techniques most webmasters start from the homepage of the website, and then design it to catch the spider's attention for a longer period of time on the homepage, so that it does not miss any part of relevant and distinctive information provided throughout the website.

Spiders start analyzing the content from the top left and moves to bottom right in a mechanical way. Therefore, it is recommended to place irrelevant information or content without keywords on the left side of the homepage. Most of the websites place advertisement and tables on the top right of the homepage, however, if these tables do not contain the keywords or relevant information, the website is mostly likely to have its ranking decrease.

Therefore, it is recommended to use the content script on the top left of the homepage; however, if the tables are placed at that position, then they should contain the relevant content to grasp the attention of spider.

It is also observed that websites using quality content along with a very captivating design are often ranked lower in the search results. This is due to the placement of irrelevant information (navigation table) prior to the relevant content. Therefore, as the spider starts working on the page, it skips that and moves to the second page unless referred back to the homepage.

For the same reason keywords and company's name is placed in the title bar so as to facilitate the spider. Spider usually takes feedback from the first paragraph and the final paragraph to judge the presence of keywords. Therefore, to obtain the maximum benefits for SEO, it is wise to provide the relevant information where spider searches it.

Linking Strategy

Links are very important while deciding the rank of the websites on Google search engine, as they are taken as a support to the website.

The dilemma is that websites focus more on the external linking strategy, which is very easy and comfortable to play with. However, they neglect to focus their attention on the internal linking strategy. Therefore, they lose their ranking in the hands of their competitor paying equal attention to internal linking strategy as well.

Therefore, most of the websites are silo structured in order to optimize the internal links for SEO. In case the website has several pages with a maximum number of internal linking, the websites will get maximum linking points by the Google spider, which usually and often results in higher ranking. Google spiders analyze the number of links on the homepage and other pages linking to the homepage for internal linking. Therefore, it is recommended to link the pages of a website with its next pages as well as the previous pages along with linking it with the homepage. For example, page A of the website should be linked to the page B of the website and the order continues and then the last page has to be linked with the page A.

There are structures with separate pages especially when looking more specifically into the silo structure, where each page of the website is a silo full of information with different sets of pages.

In that case, the home page has to be linked with each silo and then the last page of each silo has to be linked with the home page. The silo structure of a hypothetical website is explained in the Figure below as an example for better understanding.

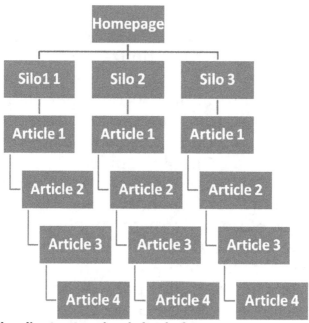

Fig: silo structured website design

The homepage of this website is linked with each of the three silos, however further links are provided within each silo among articles. Now the last article, for example, article 4 of each silo has to be connected with either to the homepage or the next silo in the website. The nature and placement of links may vary depending on the type and nature of website.

However, the objective is to generate maximum number of links in order to gain maximum points by Google spider for the linking of the website.

Internal links calculation is then used to define the Page Rank by the Google search engine, which is then used for the ranking of the website. However, if the homepage is the most important part of the website with the most relevant content, then it is advised to link all the pages of the web sites back to the home page. There are websites using this option, so that when the visitor goes to the last page, they will be provided with the option of going "back to home". These websites are designed to get maximum points for internal linking by search engine spiders.

No Follow

Keyword density varies with the quantity of the content. For example, the number of keywords for one page cannot be used effectively for two pages, as 8% for both pages is different. However, websites have to place some information on their pages which are not keywords rich. Usually privacy policy, about us, products, and price information which usually cannot and do not include the relevant keywords. Therefore, when the spider visits these pages, it finds irrelevant information.

To avoid this situation websites follow the "No follow" command in order to prevent the spider from visiting part of website with irrelevant information.

Also, certain links are placed on websites for the purpose of information. They may or may not have the relevance with the content of the website. Following such links can generate adverse results; therefore, websites try to restrict the working of Google spider for such links.

People claim that Google's spider do visit the content with "No follow" command; however, the content is not used for indexing the website or its ranking. The techniques are used for the websites with content rich information; however, exclusion of the spider is only made for the pages for irrelevant information. Otherwise, the real purpose of the search engine optimization cannot be obtained.

The technique is commonly known as Page Rank sculpting. The purpose of the techniques is to stop the spider from visiting unimportant or low value pages. However, it can be dangerous, as Google demands websites to provide pages to spider as they are viewed by the visitors. Using such techniques can affect the Page Rank as well.

Also, "no follow" is now being used as a substitute to the quality content and websites tends to provide the spider with only the useful or most relevant content. Such websites, when visited, do not perform up to the standards set by Google's search engine. This eventually hurts the reputation and image of the Google search engine. Therefore, it is expected that Google will ban such techniques in the future, which are harmful for its image. However, the technique is important in certain situations where there are websites which cannot provide all of the information to the spider, and thus has a direct affect on their ranking. However, on the other hand visitors demand such information on the same website.

Free SEO Tools

Search engine optimization has provided the business with free tools for SEO, as most of the businesses cannot afford to have search engine optimization for their websites. These free search engine optimization tools provide them with enough information and capabilities to bring websites into the higher ranking of the search engines. These tools provide the website owners with the information needed to be used for search engine optimization as on-page and off-page factors. These tools can also be used to track the performance of the websites. There are several free tools available on internet for search engine optimization, however most famous among them are:

Google analytics

Google analytics is the most used and famous tool available on internet. The friendly and reliable nature of the software has made it successful after very short time of its launch.

Very easy installation is required for the software and the software provides the necessary information about the user's who are frequently visiting the website.

Besides the frequent visits, the pattern of user behavior, information about the external links used by the visitors, location of the visitor, and time duration spent on the website is reliably calculated and provided for effective optimization. Google analytics also provide information about the words used as keywords by the visitors.

It works well for the websites that are rich in content and provide several external links. These website need to be analyzed carefully, as there are several factors involved in the development of such websites. Therefore, tools which are not capable of working with many factors produce unreliable results for such websites.

SEO Chat

SEO chat is also an online website, which provides more than 40 tools to analyze the factors for search engine optimization. However, the site offers its services of specific search engines, though Google is the most preferred one. SEO chat also provides the webmasters with the related articles and information that helps the website owners to optimize their websites. Besides the information about all the tools listed on the website, it also provides and facilitates the process of optimization.

73

Market leap website

Like Google analytics, market leap websites provide the information regarding websites that is used in search engine optimization. However, market leap websites are an online facility rather than basic software.

It provides information about three basic factors which are keyword confirmation, search engine saturation, and links.

Keyword confirmation identifies the keywords for the website and confirms as the valid keywords on the basis of its calculation. These calculations are done by calculating the number of visitors using the words as their "search word". Besides, it also provides the condition of search engines, if the search engine is saturated or operating at its maximum capacity. It is not recommended to target that search engine for the optimization of website.

The website also provides information bout the popularity of links that help websites to put the most relevant and suitable link on the website as reference. Besides, the website works well with Google search engine. It also offers a service called "university", which is available with search engine optimization articles and related information.

74

SEO Book

Learn, rank, and dominate is the positioning of the website and it true as well. Website hosts number of services including information about keywords, adverting using pay-per-click, link analysis, and ranking criteria of search engines. Besides, information provided in shape of articles and readings, website also offer a blog to learn and share experiences. Most of the services provided on the website are free, however, there are tools where others sites have to be approached. Therefore, people using those tools have to pay a certain small fee for that.

THE END

The Best Damn GOOGLE SEO Book

The next few pages are used for Search & Book Engine purposes only! The Top Google searches for the terms "Google", "SEO", "Google SEO", "Search Engine Optimization", "Optimization" "Promotion", and "Google Search Engine Optimization"

1 Seo, About Google, Activities Promotion, Ad Words, Add Url, Add Url Free, Ads By Google, Adsense, Advantage Promotions, Advertising, Advertising And Promotion, Advertising Promotion, Advertising Promotions, Adword, Adwords, Adwords Management, Adwords Optimization, Adwords Secrets, Affiliate Marketing, Affordable Search Engine Optimization, Affordable Search Engine Optimization Services, Affordable Search Engine Placement, Affordable Search Engine Submission, Affordable Seo, Affordable Seo Services, Air Force Promotion, Application Optimization, Army Promotion, Ask, Automotive Seo, Backlinks, Best Google Seo, Best Optimization, Best Search Engine Optimization, Best Seo, Better Search Engine Placement, Better Search Engine Positioning, Bid Optimization, Blog, Blog Optimization, Blogger, Bluehat Seo, Books, Books Google Com, Brand, Brand Marketing, Brand Promotion, Branding, Brands Promotion, Business, Business Letter Promotion, Business Marketing, Business Opportunities, Business Promotion, Business Promotions, Buy Seo, C Optimization, C Optimization, Calendar Google Com, Campaign Promotion, Campaigns, Cancel Google Seo, Cheap Search Engine Optimization, Cheap Seo, Check Seo, Code Optimization, Cofinimmo, Company, Competitors, Compiler Optimization, Computer Optimization, Constrained, Constrained Optimization, Constraint Optimization, Consumer Promotion, Consumer Promotions, Consumers, Content Google Seo, Content Optimization, Control Optimization, Convex Optimization, Corporate, Corporate Promotion, Creative Promotion, Creative Promotions, Customer, Customers, Customize Google, Data Optimization, David Seo, Define Optimization, Definition Of Promotion, Direct Mail, Direct Marketing, Direct Marketing Promotion, Direct Promotions, Directory, Done Seo, Doodle 4 Google, Doodle For Google, Download Google Maps, Download Google Toolbar, Dsl Engine Optimization Search, Dynamic Optimization, Earn Money, Easy Money, Easy Seo, Ebay, Ebay Com, Economical Search Engine Optimization, Effective Promotion, Effective Search Engine Optimization, Email Optimization, Engine Internet Marketing Optimization Search, Engine Marketing Optimization Search Site, Engine Optimization, Engine Optimization Techniques, Enlisted Promotion, Ethical Search Engine Optimization, Event, Event Promotion, Example Of, Example Of Promotion, Example Promotion, Exclusive Promotions, Fathom Seo, Free Advertising, Free Google Seo, Free Optimization, Free Promotion, Free Search Engine Optimization, Free Search Engine Submission, Free Seo, Free Seo Training.

The Best Damn GOOGLE SEO Book

Free Submission, Free Url Submit, Free Website Optimization, Friend, Froogle, Function Optimization, G Optimization, Gadgets Google Seo, Game Optimization, Get Rich, Get Seo, Global, Global Promotions, Gmail, Good Seo, Googie, Google, Google Ad, Google Ad Sense, Google Ad Words, Google Add, Google Ads, Google Adsense, Google Advanced Search, Google Advertising, Google Adwords, Google Adwords Seo, Google Alert, Google Analitics, Google Analytics Seo, Google Approved Seo, Google Art, Google Autofill, Google Bans Seo, Google Bar, Google Base Seo, Google Book, Google Book Search, Google C0m, Google Calculator, Google Calendars, Google Career, Google Cash, Google Certified Seo, Google Checkout, Google Co0m, Google Co9m, Google Cojm, Google Com, Google Com Ig, Google Com Seo, Google Coml, Google Cpom, Google Desktop, Google Desktop Search, Google Doc, Google Doodle, Google Doodles, Google Driving, Google Eart, Google Earth, Google Earth 2008, Google Earth 3d, Google Earth 4.2, Google Earth Free Download, Google Earth Update, Google Email, Google Erath, Google Erth, Google Es, Google Finace, Google Flash Seo, Google For Kids, Google Game, Google Gmail, Google Google, Google Google Google, Google Group, Google Groups Seo, Google Guideline For Seo, Google Hack, Google Home Page, Google Homepage, Google Image Seo, Google Improve, Google Jp, Google Lcom, Google Local Business, Google Local Seo, Google Mail, Google Map Street View, Google Maps, Google Maps For Mobile, Google Maps Mobile, Google Messenger, Google Mini, Google Movie, Google News, Google Optimization, Google Page Creator, Google People, Google Phone Book, Google Photo, Google Pinyin, Google Pop Up Blocker, Google Position, Google Profits, Google Rank, Google Ranking, Google Ranking Factors Seo, Google Ranking Factors Seo Checklist, Google Rankings, Google Real Estate, Google Report, Google Scholar Com, Google Screensaver, Google Search, Google Search Bar, Google Search Engine, Google Search Engine Marketing, Google Search Engine Optimization, Google Search Engine Optimizer, Google Search Engine Placement, Google Search Engine Ranking, Google Search Engine Submission, Google Search Engine Tips, Google Search Results, Google Search Seo, Google Sem, Google Seo, Google Seo Algorithm, Google Seo Basics, Google Seo Best Practices, Google Seo Book, Google Seo Certification, Google Seo Changes, Google Seo Company, Google Seo Domain, Google Seo Duplicate, Google Seo Experts, Google Seo Forum, Google Seo Guide, Google Seo Help, Google Seo Keyword, Google Seo Keywords, Google Seo Link, Google Seo Links, Google Seo Magic, Google Seo Magic Review, Google Seo Matt, Google Seo News, Google Seo Optimization, Google Seo Page, Google Seo Rank, Google Seo Ranking, Google Seo Rules, Google Seo Service, Google Seo Services, Google Seo Sitemap, Google Seo Software, Google Seo Supervisor, Google Seo Supervisor Trial, Google Seo Test, Google Seo Tips, Google Seo Tool, Google Seo Tools, Google Seo Training.

The Best Damn GOOGLE SEO Book

Google Seo Tutorial, Google Seo Url, Google Serps, Google Sidebar, Google Site Map, Google Space, Google Sports, Google Street, Google Street Level, Google Street Map, Google Streets, Google Streetview, Google Taiwan, Google Talk, Google Taskbar, Google Text, Google Theme, Google Themes, Google Tool, Google Tool Bar, Google Toolbar, Google Toolbar Seo, Google Toolkit, Google Tools, Google Traffic, Google Trend, Google Updater, Google Video Seo, Google Weather, Google Website, Google Widget, Google Work, Google World Map, Google's Seo, Google.com, Googles, Googles Com, Gool, Guaranteed Search Engine Marketing, Guaranteed Search Engine Optimization, Guaranteed Search Engine Placement, Guaranteed Search Engine Positioning, Guaranteed Search Engine Ranking, Guaranteed Top Search Engine Placement, Guaranteed Top Search Engine Ranking, Hat Seo Google, High Search Engine Placement, High Search Engine Positioning, High Search Engine Ranking, High Search Engine Ranking Optimization, Home Business, Hotel, Hotmail Com, Houston Search Engine Optimization, How Seo, How To Search Engine Optimization, How To Write A Promotion, How To Write Promotion, I Google, Ideas For Promotion, Igoogle, Impact Promotions, Importance Of Google In Seo, Improve Search Engine Optimization, Improve Search Engine Ranking, Improved Search Engine Placement, Increase Sales, Increase Search Engine Ranking, Increase Seo, Integer Optimization, International Search Engine Optimization, International Search Engine Placement, International Seo, Internet, Internet Advertising, Internet Marketing, Internet Marketing Seo, Internet Marketing Services, Internet Promotion, Internet Search Engine Optimization, Introduction Promotion, Invitation Promotion, It Optimization, J Seo, Jin Young, Jobs, Jobs At Google, Joe Seo, John Seo, Keyword, Keyword Optimization, Keyword Ranking, Keyword Rankings, Keyword Search, Keyword Search Engine, Keyword Search Engine Optimization, Keyword Seo, Keywords Search Engine, La Campaigne Award Promotion, Landing Page Optimization, Las Vegas Search Engine Optimization, Lcgi, Learn Search Engine Optimization, Learn Seo, Learning Seo, Letter, Letter For Promotion, Letter Of Promotion, Letter Writing, Letters, Linear Optimization, Linear Programming Optimization, Link Popularity, Link Seo, List Promotion, Local Seo, Mail Google Com, Make Money On The Internet, Making Money, Making Money Online, Management, Management Promotion, Maps, Maps Google Co, Market, Marketing, Marketing Agency, Marketing And Promotion, Marketing And Promotions, Marketing Consultants, Marketing Optimization, Marketing Plan, Marketing Plan Promotion, Marketing Promotion, Marketing Promotions, Marketing Seo, Marketing Strategies, Marketing Strategy, Marketing Website, Media Promotions, Merkey, Meta Tag Optimization, Meta Tags, Mobile, Mobile Seo, Msn, Natural Search Engine Optimization, Need Seo, Negative Seo, New Google Seo, New Seo, News Google Com, Nigritude Ultramarine, Nonlinear Optimization, Objectives.

Of Google In Seo, Off Page Optimization, Officer Promotion, On Page Optimization, Online Advertising, Online Business, Online Marketing, Online Money, Online Promotion, Online Promotions, Online Seo, Optimisation, Optimization, Optimization Algorithm, Optimization Algorithms, Optimization Analysis, Optimization Applications, Optimization Approach, Optimization Articles, Optimization Based, Optimization Book, Optimization Com, Optimization Companies, Optimization Constraints, Optimization Consultant, Optimization Engine, Optimization Example, Optimization Examples, Optimization Experts, Optimization Firms, Optimization Forum, Optimization In R, Optimization Keywords, Optimization Marketing Service Solution, Optimization Method, Optimization Methods, Optimization Model, Optimization Modeling, Optimization Models, Optimization Online, Optimization Placement, Optimization Ppt, Optimization Problem, Optimization Problems, Optimization Report, Optimization Search Technique, Optimization Service Center, Optimization Services, Optimization Solution, Optimization Specialist, Optimization Strategies, Optimization Techniques, Optimization Test, Optimization Theory, Optimization Tips, Optimization Tool, Optimization Tools, Optimization World, Optimizations, Optimize, Optimize Search Engine, Optimize Website, Optimizer, Optimizing, Organic Search Engine Optimization, Organic Search Optimization, Organic Seo, Page Optimization, Page Rank, Page Seo, Paid Search Engine Placement, Paid Search Marketing, Pay For Placement Search Engine, Pay Per Click, Pay Per Click Online Positioning, Pay Per Click Optimization, Pay Per Click Placement, Pdf Optimization, Performance Optimization, Photo Optimization, Picasaweb Google Com, Placement, Positioning, Positive Promotion, Ppc, Ppc Management, Ppc Marketing, Ppc Optimization, Ppc Search Engine Placement, Ppc Search Engines, Price Optimization, Pricing, Pricing Optimization, Print Optimization, Product, Product Promotion, Product Promotions, Products, Professional Search Engine Optimization, Programming Optimization, Promo, Promote, Promoters, Promoting, Promotion, Promotion Agencies, Promotion Agency, Promotion Analysis, Promotion Announcement, Promotion Board, Promotion Branding, Promotion Campaigns, Promotion Codes, Promotion Com, Promotion Communication, Promotion Communications, Promotion Companies, Promotion Company, Promotion Criteria, Promotion Customer, Promotion Distribution, Promotion Examples, Promotion Global, Promotion Ideas, Promotion Industry, Promotion Letter, Promotion Letter Writing, Promotion Letters, Promotion Manager, Promotion Market, Promotion Marketing Association, Promotion Media, Promotion Mix, Promotion Objectives, Promotion Optimization, Promotion Planning, Promotion Ppt, Promotion Pricing, Promotion Products, Promotion Results, Promotion Retail, Promotion Sample, Promotion Strategic, Promotion Strategies, Promotion Strategy.

Promotion Template, Promotion Tools, Promotion Wars, Promotion Writing, Promotional, Promotional Advertising, Promotional Campaign, Promotional Companies, Promotional Company, Promotional Concepts, Promotional Gift, Promotional Gifts, Promotional Item, Promotional Items, Promotional Letter, Promotional Marketing, Promotional Materials, Promotional Merchandise, Promotional Mix, Promotional Pens, Promotional Product, Promotional Products, Promotional Products Industry, Promotional Sales, Promotional Strategies, Promotional Strategy, Promotions, Promotions Com, Promotions Companies, Promotions Company, Promotions Director, Promotions Now, Promotions Plus, Public Relations, Public Relations Promotion, Quadratic Optimization, Rank Optimization, Ranking Optimization, Ranking Service Top Search Engine, Real Estate Search Engine Optimization, Request Promotion, Research Promotion, Retail Promotions, Sales, Sales Promotion, Sales Promotion Ideas, Sales Promotions, Samples Promotion, Scheduling Optimization, Se Optimization, Seach Engine Optimization, Search, Search Engin Optimization, Search Engine, Search Engine Advertising, Search Engine Best, Search Engine Cloaker, Search Engine Consultant, Search Engine Consultants, Search Engine Listing, Search Engine Listings, Search Engine Marketing, Search Engine Marketing Companies, Search Engine Marketing Company, Search Engine Marketing Pro, Search Engine Marketing Tool, Search Engine Optimisation, Search Engine Optimisation Services, Search Engine Optimization, Search Engine Optimization Advertising, Search Engine Optimization Advice, Search Engine Optimization Agency, Search Engine Optimization Analysis, Search Engine Optimization And Seo, Search Engine Optimization And Seo Services, Search Engine Optimization And Submission, Search Engine Optimization And Submission Services, Search Engine Optimization Articles, Search Engine Optimization Book, Search Engine Optimization Books, Search Engine Optimization Certification, Search Engine Optimization Check, Search Engine Optimization Classes, Search Engine Optimization Companies, Search Engine Optimization Company, Search Engine Optimization Consultant, Search Engine Optimization Consultants, Search Engine Optimization Consulting, Search Engine Optimization Content, Search Engine Optimization Copywriting, Search Engine Optimization Cost, Search Engine Optimization Expert, Search Engine Optimization Experts, Search Engine Optimization Firm, Search Engine Optimization Firms, Search Engine Optimization For Dummies, Search Engine Optimization Forum, Search Engine Optimization Forums, Search Engine Optimization Free, Search Engine Optimization Google, Search Engine Optimization Guide, Search Engine Optimization Help, Search Engine Optimization How, Search Engine Optimization Information, Search Engine Optimization Jobs, Search Engine Optimization Key Words, Search Engine Optimization Keywords.

Search Engine Optimization Made Easy, Search Engine Optimization Marketing, Search Engine Optimization Meta, Search Engine Optimization Meta Tags, Search Engine Optimization News, Search Engine Optimization Page, Search Engine Optimization Pay Per Click, Search Engine Optimization Pricing, Search Engine Optimization Pro, Search Engine Optimization Program, Search Engine Optimization Promotion, Search Engine Optimization Rankings, Search Engine Optimization Report, Search Engine Optimization Results, Search Engine Optimization Secrets, Search Engine Optimization Seo, Search Engine Optimization Seo Services, Search Engine Optimization Service, Search Engine Optimization Services, Search Engine Optimization Software, Search Engine Optimization Specalist, Search Engine Optimization Specialist, Search Engine Optimization Specialists, Search Engine Optimization Strategies, Search Engine Optimization Strategy, Search Engine Optimization Technique, Search Engine Optimization Techniques, Search Engine Optimization Tip, Search Engine Optimization Tips, Search Engine Optimization Tool, Search Engine Optimization Tools, Search Engine Optimization Training, Search Engine Optimization Tutorial, Search Engine Optimization Tutorials, Search Engine Optimization Url, Search Engine Optimization Web Site, Search Engine Optimizer, Search Engine Optimizers, Search Engine Optimizing, Search Engine Pay Per Click, Search Engine Placement, Search Engine Placement Companies, Search Engine Placement Firm, Search Engine Placement Improvement, Search Engine Placement Optimization, Search Engine Placement Specialist, Search Engine Position, Search Engine Position Optimization, Search Engine Position Placement, Search Engine Position Ranking, Search Engine Positioning, Search Engine Positioning Firm, Search Engine Positioning Tool, Search Engine Ppc, Search Engine Promotion, Search Engine Promotion Services, Search Engine Rank, Search Engine Rank Optimization, Search Engine Ranking, Search Engine Ranking Improvement, Search Engine Ranking Optimization, Search Engine Ranking Software, Search Engine Ranking Specialist, Search Engine Ranking Tool, Search Engine Rankings, Search Engine Registration, Search Engine Secrets, Search Engine Seo, Search Engine Services, Search Engine Submission, Search Engine Submission Firm, Search Engine Submission Optimization, Search Engine Submission Positioning, Search Engine Submission Services, Search Engine Submission Tools, Search Engine Submissions, Search Engine Submit, Search Engine Tips, Search Engine Traffic, Search Engines, Search Engines Optimization, Search Marketing, Search Optimisation, Search Optimization, Search Ranking, Segmentation, Selling Promotion, Sem, Seo, Seo Administrator, Seo Advice, Seo Agency, Seo And Google, Seo Article, Seo Black, Seo Blog, Seo Book, Seo Books, Seo By Google, Seo Checklist, Seo Com, Seo Companies, Seo Companies Usa, Seo Company, Seo Consultant, Seo Consultants, Seo Consultation, Seo Consulting, Seo Content, Seo Contest, Seo Copy.

81

The Best Damn GOOGLE SEO Book

Seo Copywriting, Seo Course, Seo Courses, Seo D Urgell, Seo Directory, Seo Elite, Seo Elite 4, Seo Evaluation, Seo Expert, Seo Experts, Seo Firm, Seo Firms, Seo For Google, Seo Forum, Seo Forums, Seo G, Seo Google Index, Seo Guaranteed, Seo Guide, Seo Guy, Seo H1, Seo Help, Seo Hyun Jin, Seo Images, Seo In Google, Seo Inc, Seo Info, Seo Information, Seo Japanese, Seo Jin Young, Seo Jobs, Seo Keyword, Seo Keywords, Seo Links, Seo List, Seo Magic, Seo Marketing, Seo Master, Seo News, Seo Note, Seo On Google, Seo Optimisation, Seo Optimization, Seo Optimized, Seo Org, Seo Pack, Seo Pdf, Seo Placement, Seo Plan, Seo Press Release, Seo Press Releases, Seo Price, Seo Pricing, Seo Pro, Seo Process, Seo Program, Seo Project, Seo Promotion, Seo Pros, Seo Questions, Seo Rank, Seo Ranking, Seo Rankings, Seo Report, Seo Reporting, Seo Resource, Seo Review, Seo Reviews, Seo Roundtable, Seo Search, Seo Search Engine, Seo Search Engine Optimization, Seo Seminar, Seo Serps, Seo Service, Seo Services, Seo Software, Seo Solution, Seo Specialist, Seo Specialists, Seo Sponsors For Educational Opportunity, Seo Spyglass, Seo Standards, Seo Statistics, Seo Strategy, Seo Submission, Seo Suite, Seo Taeji, Seo Tai Ji, Seo Taiji, Seo Taji, Seo Techniques, Seo Tip, Seo Tips, Seo Tips For Google, Seo To Google, Seo Tool, Seo Toolkit, Seo Tools, Seo Training, Seo Tutorial, Seo U, Seo Uk, Seo Usa, Seo Usa Org, Seo Web Design, Seo Website, Seo With Google, Seo Workshop, Seo World, Seo Writers, Seo Writing, Seo Yeon, Seo Young, Seo Young Eun, Seo 対策, Seochat, Seraphim Proudleduck, Serps, Service Optimization, Sim64, Simplex Optimization, Site Optimization, Site Optimization Firm, Site Promotion, Site Search Engine Optimization, Small Business Seo, Sponsors For Educational Opportunity, Sql Optimization, Stochastic Optimization, Strategies, Strategy, Su Jine, Submission Optimization, Submit Search Engine Free, Submit To Search Engines, Submit Url, Success, Success Promotion, Successful Promotion, Successful Promotions, Successful Promotions Magazine, Superior Optimization, Systems Optimization, Tai Ji, Techniques Promotion, The Best Seo, The Promotion, Titan Seo, Toolbar, Top 10 Optimization, Top 10 Search Engine Optimization, Top 10 Search Engine Placement, Top Google Seo, Top Optimization, Top Search Engine, Top Search Engine Marketing, Top Search Engine Optimization, Top Search Engine Placement, Top Search Engine Placement Services, Top Search Engine Position, Top Search Engine Positioning, Top Search Engine Ranking, Top Seo, Trade Promotion Management, Trade Promotions, Traffic Optimization, Trafficseeker, Trellian, Trellian Seo, Tv Optimization, Unconstrained Optimization, Usa Seo Pros, Utorrent Optimization, Video, Video Google Com, Video Search Engine Optimization, Video Seo, Vista Optimization, Vista Optimization Guide, Web Analytics, Web Design, Web Design Company, Web Design Search Engine Optimization, Web Design Services, Web Development, Web Marketing, Web Marketing Search Engine Optimization, Web Optimization.

Web Page Optimization, Web Page Search Engine Optimization, Web Promotion, Web Search Engine Optimization, Web Site, Web Site Design, Web Site Optimization, Web Site Promotion, Web Site Ranking, Web Site Seo, Webhosting, Website, Website Marketing, Website Optimisation, Website Optimization, Website Optimization Companies, Website Positioning, Website Promotion, Website Ranking, Website Rankings, Website Search Engine Optimization, Website Seo, Website Submission, Website Submission Optimization, Website Submit, What Is An Seo, Why Seo, Word Optimization, Work For Google, Work From Home, World Promotions, Wp Seo, Ww Google Com, Www Docs Google Com, Www Google C Om, Www Google Ccom, Www Google Cdom, Www Google Cm, Www Google CoOm, Www Google Cocm, Www Google Coim, Www Google Cojm, Www Google Cokm, Www Google Com, Www Google Conm, Www Google Coom, Www Google Cp, Www Google Cpom, Www Google Cvom, Www Google Earth, Www Google Earth Com, Www Google Xom, Www Googles Com, Www Map Google Com, Www Maps Google Com, Www Seo, Www.google.com, You Tube, Young Eun, Youtube, Youtube Seo.

The common miss spellings of the terms Google, Seo, Google Seo, Optimization, Search Engine Optimization, Google Search Engine Optimization, and Promotion

Google, Oogle, Gogle, Goole, Googe, Googl, Ogogle, Gogole, Goolge, Googel, Ggoogle, Gooogle, Googgle, Googlle, Googlee, Foogle, Hoogle, Giogle, Gpogle, Goigle, Gopgle, Goofle, Goohle, Googke, Goog;e, Googlw, Googlr, Toogle, Yoogle, Boogle, Voogle, G9ogle, G0ogle, Glogle, Gkogle, Go9gle, Go0gle, Golgle, Gokgle, Gootle, Gooyle, Gooble, Goovle, Googoe, Googpe, Goog.e, Goog,e, Googl3, Googl4, Googld, Googls, Seo, Eo, So, Se, Eso, Soe, Sseo, Seeo, Seoo, Aeo, Deo, Swo, Sro, Sei, Sep, Weo, Eeo, Xeo, Zeo, S3o, S4o, Sdo, Sso, Se9, Se0, Sel, Sek, Google Seo, Googleseo, Seo Google, Oogle Seo, Gogle Seo, Goole Seo, Googe Seo, Googl Seo, Google Eo, Google So, Google Se, Ogogle Seo, Gogole Seo, Goolge Seo, Googel Seo, Google Eso, Google Soe, Ggoogle Seo, Gooogle Seo, Googgle Seo, Googlle Seo, Googlee Seo, Google Sseo, Google Seeo, Google Seoo, Foogle Seo, Hoogle Seo, Giogle Seo, Gpogle Seo, Goigle Seo, Gopgle Seo, Goofle Seo, Goohle Seo, Googke Seo, Goog;e Seo, Googlw Seo, Googlr Seo, Google Aeo, Google Deo, Google Swo, Google Sro, Google Sei, Google Sep, Toogle Seo, Yoogle Seo, Boogle Seo, Voogle Seo, G9ogle Seo, G0ogle Seo, Glogle Seo, Gkogle Seo, Go9gle Seo, Go0gle Seo, Golgle Seo, Gokgle Seo, Gootle Seo, Gooyle Seo, Gooble Seo, Goovle Seo, Googoe Seo, Googpe Seo, Goog.e Seo, Goog,e Seo, Googl3 Seo, Googl4 Seo, Googld Seo, Googls Seo, Google Weo, Google Eeo, Google Xeo, Google Zeo, Google S3o, Google S4o, Google Sdo, Google Sso, Google Se9, Google Se0, Google Sel, Google Sek, Optimization, Ptimization, Otimization, Opimization, Optmization, Optiization, Optimzation.

83

Optimiation, Optimiztion, Optimizaion, Optimizaton, Optimizatin, Optimizatio, Potimization, Otpimization, Opitmization, Optmiization, Optiimzation, Optimziation, Optimiaztion, Optimiztaion, Optimizaiton, Optimizatoin, Optimizatino, Ooptimization, Opptimization, Opttimization, Optiimization, Optimmization, Optimiization, Optimizzation, Optimizaation, Optimizattion, Optimizatiion, Optimizatioon, Optimizationn, Iptimization, Pptimization, Oprimization, Opyimization, Optumization, Optomization, Optinization, Opti,ization, Optimuzation, Optimozation, Optimixation, Optimizstion, Optimizarion, Optimizayion, Optimizatuon, Optimizatoon, Optimizatiin, Optimizatipn, Optimizatiob, Optimizatiom, 9ptimization, 0ptimization, Lptimization, Kptimization, Op5imization, Op6imization, Opgimization, Opfimization, Opt8mization, Opt9mization, Optkmization, Optjmization, Optijization, Optikization, Optim8zation, Optim9zation, Optimkzation, Optimjzation, Optimiaation, Optimisation, Optimizqtion, Optimizwtion, Optimizztion, Optimiza5ion, Optimiza6ion, Optimizagion, Optimizafion, Optimizat8on, Optimizat9on, Optimizatkon, Optimizatjon, Optimizati9n, Optimizati0n, Optimizatiln, Optimizatikn, Optimizatioh, Optimizatioj, Search Engine Optimization, Searchengine Optimization, Search Engineoptimization, Searchengineoptimization, Search Optimization Engine, Engine Search Optimization, Engine Optimization Search, Optimization Search Engine, Optimization Engine Search, Earch Engine Optimization, Sarch Engine Optimization, Serch Engine Optimization, Seach Engine Optimization, Searh Engine Optimization, Searc Engine Optimization, Search Ngine Optimization, Search Egine Optimization, Search Enine Optimization, Search Engne Optimization, Search Engie Optimization, Search Engin Optimization, Search Engine Ptimization, Search Engine Otimization, Search Engine Opimization, Search Engine Optmization, Search Engine Optiization, Search Engine Optimzation, Search Engine Optimiation, Search Engine Optimiztion, Search Engine Optimizaion, Search Engine Optimizaton, Search Engine Optimizatin, Search Engine Optimizatio, Esarch Engine Optimization, Saerch Engine Optimization, Serach Engine Optimization, Seacrh Engine Optimization, Searhc Engine Optimization, Search Negine Optimization, Search Egnine Optimization, Search Enigne Optimization, Search Engnie Optimization, Search Engien Optimization, Search Engine Potimization, Search Engine Otpimization, Search Engine Opitmization, Search Engine Optmiization, Search Engine Optiimzation, Search Engine Optimziation, Search Engine Optimiaztion, Search Engine Optimiztaion, Search Engine Optimizaiton, Search Engine Optimizatoin, Search Engine Optimizatino, Ssearch Engine Optimization, Seearch Engine Optimization, Seaarch Engine Optimization, Searrch Engine Optimization, Searcch Engine Optimization, Searchh Engine Optimization, Search Eengine Optimization, Search Enngine Optimization, Search Enggine Optimization.

Search Engiine Optimization, Search Enginne Optimization, Search Enginee Optimization, Search Engine Ooptimization, Search Engine Opptimization, Search Engine Opttimization, Search Engine Optiimization, Search Engine Optimmization, Search Engine Optimiization, Search Engine Optimizzation, Search Engine Optimizaation, Search Engine Optimizattion, Search Engine Optimizatiion, Search Engine Optimizatioon, Search Engine Optimizationn, Aearch Engine Optimization, Dearch Engine Optimization, Swarch Engine Optimization, Srarch Engine Optimization, Sesrch Engine Optimization, Seaech Engine Optimization, Seatch Engine Optimization, Searxh Engine Optimization, Searvh Engine Optimization, Searcg Engine Optimization, Searcj Engine Optimization, Search Wngine Optimization, Search Rngine Optimization, Search Ebgine Optimization, Search Emgine Optimization, Search Enfine Optimization, Search Enhine Optimization, Search Engune Optimization, Search Engone Optimization, Search Engibe Optimization, Search Engime Optimization, Search Enginw Optimization, Search Enginr Optimization, Search Engine Iptimization, Search Engine Pptimization, Search Engine Oprimization, Search Engine Opyimization, Search Engine Optumization, Search Engine Optomization, Search Engine Optinization, Search Engine Opti,ization, Search Engine Optimuzation, Search Engine Optimozation, Search Engine Optimixation, Search Engine Optimizstion, Search Engine Optimizarion, Search Engine Optimizayion, Search Engine Optimizatuon, Search Engine Optimizatoon, Search Engine Optimizatiin, Search Engine Optimizatipn, Search Engine Optimizatiob, Search Engine Optimizatiom, Wearch Engine Optimization, Eearch Engine Optimization, Xearch Engine Optimization, Zearch Engine Optimization, S3arch Engine Optimization, S4arch Engine Optimization, Sdarch Engine Optimization, Ssarch Engine Optimization, Seqrch Engine Optimization, Sewrch Engine Optimization, Sezrch Engine Optimization, Sea4ch Engine Optimization, Sea5ch Engine Optimization, Seafch Engine Optimization, Seadch Engine Optimization, Seardh Engine Optimization, Searfh Engine Optimization, Searcy Engine Optimization, Searcu Engine Optimization, Searcn Engine Optimization, Searcb Engine Optimization, Search 3ngine Optimization, Search 4ngine Optimization, Search Dngine Optimization, Search Sngine Optimization, Search Ehgine Optimization, Search Ejgine Optimization, Search Entine Optimization, Search Enyine Optimization, Search Enbine Optimization, Search Envine Optimization, Search Eng8ne Optimization, Search Eng9ne Optimization, Search Engkne Optimization, Search Engjne Optimization, Search Engihe Optimization, Search Engije Optimization, Search Engin3 Optimization, Search Engin4 Optimization, Search Engind Optimization, Search Engins Optimization, Search Engine 9ptimization, Search Engine 0ptimization, Search Engine Lptimization, Search Engine Kptimization, Search Engine Op5imization, Search Engine Op6imization, Search Engine Opgimization, Search Engine Opfimization.

Search Engine Opt8mization, Search Engine Opt9mization, Search Engine Optkmization, Search Engine Optjmization, Search Engine Optijization, Search Engine Optikization, Search Engine Optim8zation, Search Engine Optim9zation, Search Engine Optimkzation, Search Engine Optimjzation, Search Engine Optimiaation, Search Engine Optimisation, Search Engine Optimizqtion, Search Engine Optimizwtion, Search Engine Optimizztion, Search Engine Optimiza5ion, Search Engine Optimiza6ion, Search Engine Optimizagion, Search Engine Optimizafion, Search Engine Optimizat8on, Search Engine Optimizat9on, Search Engine Optimizatkon, Search Engine Optimizatjon, Search Engine Optimizati9n, Search Engine Optimizati0n, Search Engine Optimizatiln, Search Engine Optimizatikn, Search Engine Optimizatioh, Search Engine Optimizatioj, Google Search Engine Optimization, Googlesearch Engine Optimization, Google Searchengine Optimization, Google Search Engineoptimization, Googlesearchengine Optimization, Googlesearch Engineoptimization, Google Searchengineoptimization, Googlesearchengineoptimization, Google Search Optimization Engine, Google Engine Search Optimization, Google Engine Optimization Search, Google Optimization Search Engine, Google Optimization Engine Search, Search Google Engine Optimization, Search Google Optimization Engine, Search Engine Google Optimization, Search Engine Optimization Google, Search Optimization Google Engine, Search Optimization Engine Google, Engine Google Search Optimization, Engine Google Optimization Search, Engine Search Google Optimization, Engine Search Optimization Google, Engine Optimization Google Search, Engine Optimization Search Google, Optimization Google Search Engine, Optimization Google Engine Search, Optimization Search Google Engine, Optimization Search Engine Google, Optimization Engine Google Search, Optimization Engine Search Google, Oogle Search Engine Optimization, Gogle Search Engine Optimization, Goole Search Engine Optimization, Googe Search Engine Optimization, Googl Search Engine Optimization, Google Earch Engine Optimization, Google Sarch Engine Optimization, Google Serch Engine Optimization, Google Seach Engine Optimization, Google Searh Engine Optimization, Google Searc Engine Optimization, Google Search Ngine Optimization, Google Search Egine Optimization, Google Search Enine Optimization, Google Search Engne Optimization, Google Search Engie Optimization, Google Search Engin Optimization, Google Search Engine Ptimization, Google Search Engine Otimization, Google Search Engine Opimization, Google Search Engine Optmization, Google Search Engine Optiization, Google Search Engine Optimzation, Google Search Engine Optimiation, Google Search Engine Optimiztion, Google Search Engine Optimizaion, Google Search Engine Optimizaton, Google Search Engine Optimizatin, Google Search Engine Optimizatio, Ogogle Search Engine Optimization.

The Best Damn GOOGLE SEO Book

Gogole Search Engine Optimization, Goolge Search Engine Optimization, Googel Search Engine Optimization, Google Esarch Engine Optimization, Google Saerch Engine Optimization, Google Serach Engine Optimization, Google Seacrh Engine Optimization, Google Searhc Engine Optimization, Google Search Negine Optimization, Google Search Egnine Optimization, Google Search Enigne Optimization, Google Search Engnie Optimization, Google Search Engien Optimization, Google Search Engine Potimization, Google Search Engine Otpimization, Google Search Engine Opitmization, Google Search Engine Optmiization, Google Search Engine Optiimzation, Google Search Engine Optimziation, Google Search Engine Optimiaztion, Google Search Engine Optimiztaion, Google Search Engine Optimizaiton, Google Search Engine Optimizatoin, Google Search Engine Optimizatino, Ggoogle Search Engine Optimization, Gooogle Search Engine Optimization, Googgle Search Engine Optimization, Googlle Search Engine Optimization, Googlee Search Engine Optimization, Google Ssearch Engine Optimization, Google Seearch Engine Optimization, Google Seaarch Engine Optimization, Google Searrch Engine Optimization, Google Searcch Engine Optimization, Google Searchh Engine Optimization, Google Search Eengine Optimization, Google Search Enngine Optimization, Google Search Enggine Optimization, Google Search Engiine Optimization, Google Search Enginne Optimization, Google Search Enginee Optimization, Google Search Engine Ooptimization, Google Search Engine Opptimization, Google Search Engine Opttimization, Google Search Engine Optiimization, Google Search Engine Optimmization, Google Search Engine Optimiization, Google Search Engine Optimizzation, Google Search Engine Optimizaation, Google Search Engine Optimizattion, Google Search Engine Optimizatiion, Google Search Engine Optimizatioon, Google Search Engine Optimizationn, Foogle Search Engine Optimization, Hoogle Search Engine Optimization, Giogle Search Engine Optimization, Gpogle Search Engine Optimization, Goigle Search Engine Optimization, Gopgle Search Engine Optimization, Goofle Search Engine Optimization, Goohle Search Engine Optimization, Googke Search Engine Optimization, Goog;e Search Engine Optimization, Googlw Search Engine Optimization, Googlr Search Engine Optimization, Google Aearch Engine Optimization, Google Dearch Engine Optimization, Google Swarch Engine Optimization, Google Srarch Engine Optimization, Google Sesrch Engine Optimization, Google Seaech Engine Optimization, Google Seatch Engine Optimization, Google Searxh Engine Optimization, Google Searvh Engine Optimization, Google Searcg Engine Optimization, Google Searcj Engine Optimization, Google Search Wngine Optimization, Google Search Rngine Optimization, Google Search Ebgine Optimization, Google Search Emgine Optimization, Google Search Enfine Optimization, Google Search Enhine Optimization.

87

Google Search Engune Optimization, Google Search Engone Optimization, Google Search Engibe Optimization, Google Search Engime Optimization, Google Search Enginw Optimization, Google Search Enginr Optimization, Google Search Engine Iptimization, Google Search Engine Pptimization, Google Search Engine Oprimization, Google Search Engine Opyimization, Google Search Engine Optumization, Google Search Engine Optomization, Google Search Engine Optinization, Google Search Engine Opti,ization, Google Search Engine Optimuzation, Google Search Engine Optimozation, Google Search Engine Optimixation, Google Search Engine Optimizstion, Google Search Engine Optimizarion, Google Search Engine Optimizayion, Google Search Engine Optimizatuon, Google Search Engine Optimizatoon, Google Search Engine Optimizatiin, Google Search Engine Optimizatipn, Google Search Engine Optimizatiob, Google Search Engine Optimizatiom, Toogle Search Engine Optimization, Yoogle Search Engine Optimization, Boogle Search Engine Optimization, Voogle Search Engine Optimization, G9ogle Search Engine Optimization, G0ogle Search Engine Optimization, Glogle Search Engine Optimization, Gkogle Search Engine Optimization, Go9gle Search Engine Optimization, Go0gle Search Engine Optimization, Golgle Search Engine Optimization, Gokgle Search Engine Optimization, Gootle Search Engine Optimization, Gooyle Search Engine Optimization, Gooble Search Engine Optimization, Goovle Search Engine Optimization, Googoe Search Engine Optimization, Googpe Search Engine Optimization, Goog.e Search Engine Optimization, Goog,e Search Engine Optimization, Googl3 Search Engine Optimization, Googl4 Search Engine Optimization, Googld Search Engine Optimization, Googls Search Engine Optimization, Google Wearch Engine Optimization, Google Eearch Engine Optimization, Google Xearch Engine Optimization, Google Zearch Engine Optimization, Google S3arch Engine Optimization, Google S4arch Engine Optimization, Google Sdarch Engine Optimization, Google Ssarch Engine Optimization, Google Seqrch Engine Optimization, Google Sewrch Engine Optimization, Google Sezrch Engine Optimization, Google Sea4ch Engine Optimization, Google Sea5ch Engine Optimization, Google Seafch Engine Optimization, Google Seadch Engine Optimization, Google Seardh Engine Optimization, Google Searfh Engine Optimization, Google Searcy Engine Optimization, Google Searcu Engine Optimization, Google Searcn Engine Optimization, Google Searcb Engine Optimization, Google Search 3ngine Optimization, Google Search 4ngine Optimization, Google Search Dngine Optimization, Google Search Sngine Optimization, Google Search Ehgine Optimization, Google Search Ejgine Optimization, Google Search Entine Optimization, Google Search Enyine Optimization, Google Search Enbine Optimization, Google Search Envine Optimization, Google Search Eng8ne Optimization.

Google Search Eng9ne Optimization, Google Search Engkne Optimization, Google Search Engjne Optimization, Google Search Engihe Optimization, Google Search Engije Optimization, Google Search Engin3 Optimization, Google Search Engin4 Optimization, Google Search Engind Optimization, Google Search Engins Optimization, Google Search Engine 9ptimization, Google Search Engine 0ptimization, Google Search Engine Lptimization, Google Search Engine Kptimization, Google Search Engine Op5imization, Google Search Engine Op6imization, Google Search Engine Opgimization, Google Search Engine Opfimization, Google Search Engine Opt8mization, Google Search Engine Opt9mization, Google Search Engine Optkmization, Google Search Engine Optjmization, Google Search Engine Optijization, Google Search Engine Optikization, Google Search Engine Optim8zation, Google Search Engine Optim9zation, Google Search Engine Optimkzation, Google Search Engine Optimjzation, Google Search Engine Optimiaation, Google Search Engine Optimisation, Google Search Engine Optimizqtion, Google Search Engine Optimizwtion, Google Search Engine Optimizztion, Google Search Engine Optimiza5ion, Google Search Engine Optimiza6ion, Google Search Engine Optimizagion, Google Search Engine Optimizafion, Google Search Engine Optimizat8on, Google Search Engine Optimizat9on, Google Search Engine Optimizatkon, Google Search Engine Optimizatjon, Google Search Engine Optimizati9n, Google Search Engine Optimizati0n, Google Search Engine Optimizatiln, Google Search Engine Optimizatikn, Google Search Engine Optimizatioh, Google Search Engine Optimizatioj, Promotion, Romotion, Pomotion, Prmotion, Prootion, Promtion, Promoion, Promoton, Promotin, Promotio, Rpomotion, Pormotion, Prmootion, Proomtion, Promtoion, Promoiton, Promotoin, Promotino, Ppromotion, Prromotion, Proomotion, Prommotion, Promootion, Promottion, Promotiion, Promotioon, Promotionn, Peomotion, Ptomotion, Primotion, Prpmotion, Pronotion, Pro,otion, Promition, Promption, Promorion, Promoyion, Promotuon, Promotoon, Promotiin, Promotipn, Promotiob, Promotiom, P4omotion, P5omotion, Pfomotion, Pdomotion, Pr9motion, Pr0motion, Prlmotion, Prkmotion, Projotion, Prokotion, Prom9tion, Prom0tion, Promltion, Promktion, Promo5ion, Promo6ion, Promogion, Promofion, Promot8on, Promot9on, Promotkon, Promotjon, Promoti9n, Promoti0n, Promotiln, Promotikn, Promotioh, Promotioj.

The Best Damn GOOGLE SEO Book

Books > Computers & Internet > Web Development > Web Services
Books > Computers & Internet > Home Computing > Internet > Online Searching
Books > Computers & Internet > Business & Culture > Web Marketing

Business & Investing > General
Computers & Internet > Business & Culture > Web Marketing
Computers & Internet > General
Computers & Internet > Home Computing > Internet > Online Searching
Computers & Internet > Web Development > Web Services

- Business & Management
- Web browsers
- Computer networks
- Online Searching
- Business & Economics
- Business / Economics / Finance
- Business/Economics
- Business & Economics / E-Commerce / Internet Marketing
- E-Commerce - Internet Marketing
- Online Services - General
- Web - General
- Internet marketing
- Internet searching
- Web search engines
- Computing: General

www.ingramcontent.com/pod-product-compliance
Lightning Source LLC
LaVergne TN
LVHW052309060326
832902LV00021B/3782